636.9     Anders, Rebecca
A          Winslow the hamster.    Minneapolis,
     Minn., Carolrhoda Bks., 1976.
         unp.   illus. draws. photos. (part col.)
c.1

    1. Hamsters   I. Title

# Winslow
# the
# Hamster

*The Animal Friends Books*

# Winslow
# the
# Hamster

by
**Rebecca Anders**

CAROLRHODA BOOKS
MINNEAPOLIS, MINNESOTA U.S.A

Revised English text by Rebecca Anders. Original French
text by Anne-Marie Pajot. Translation by Dyan Hammar-
berg. Photographs by Rank. Drawings by L'Enc Matte.

LIBRARY OF CONGRESS CATALOGING IN PUBLICATION DATA

Anders, Rebecca.
    Winslow the hamster.

    (The Animal Friends Books)
    Original ed. published under title: Gaspard le hamster.
    SUMMARY: Two friends discover the world of hamsters,
small nocturnal rodents that make interesting pets.

    1. Hamsters as pets—Juvenile literature. [1. Hamsters]
I. Pajot, Anne Marie. Gaspard le hamster.  II. Rank.
III. Matte, L'Enc.  IV. Title.

SF459.H3A46 1977            636'.93'234            76-40966
ISBN 0-87614-078-9

First published in the United States of America 1977 by
Carolrhoda Books, Inc. All English language rights reserved.

Original edition published by Librairie A. Hatier, Paris,
France under the title GASPARD LE HAMSTER.
English text and drawings © 1977 Carolrhoda Books, Inc.
Photographs © 1969 Librairie A. Hatier.

Manufactured in the United States of America.
Published simultaneously in Canada by J. M. Dent & Sons
(Canada) Ltd., Don Mills, Ontario.

International Standard Book Number: 0-87614-078-9
Library of Congress Catalog Card Number: 76-40966

1  2  3  4  5  6  7  8  9  10  85  84  83  82  81  80  79  78  77

Michael has a brand-new pet. His pet is a tiny ball of fur that likes to hunt for sunflower seeds in Michael's pockets. It has shiny black eyes and ears as soft as velvet. It is so small that it can ride on Michael's hand or hide in Grandfather Winslow's old straw hat. And it straightens its whiskers with tiny pink paws that look almost like human hands.

Is Michael's new pet a chipmunk? Is it a mouse? No, this furry little creature is a hamster, and its name is Winslow. Michael named his pet after Grandfather Winslow, whose hat the hamster likes so well.

Winslow is a friendly, clever animal who knows just how to win treats from Michael. All Winslow has to do to get sunflower seeds is to peek out from under Grandfather's hat or stand up on his hind legs. And Winslow, greedy fellow that he is, takes more seeds than he can eat at one time! Some seeds go to Winslow's stomach, while others are tucked away in his cheek pouches.

Michael's friend Shermie is amazed at how much food Winslow can store in his cheek pouches. "I wish I could do the same thing with cupcakes and gumdrops," says Shermie. "But then I would look as chubby as Winslow."

Michael is quick to explain that Winslow doesn't stay chubby-looking for long. "Once Winslow is back in his cage, he spits all the food out of his pouches and stores it." Michael goes on to tell Shermie that the word "hamster" comes from the German word *hamstern*, which means "to hoard" or "to store."

"Winslow's wild relatives in Europe used to steal the farmers' grain and store it in their burrows," says Michael. "One wild hamster could store as much as 70 pounds of seeds for the winter. But the farmers didn't like the wild hamsters stealing their grain," he says, "so most of them were killed."

"Where do the tame hamsters come from, then?" wonders Shermie. But before Michael can reply, Winslow is begging for another treat. Michael makes him reach for a sunflower seed, but Winslow still is not satisfied. He looks here, then there. He even peeks in Michael's nose, but no treat.

Michael finally gives Winslow a whole pile of sunflower seeds. Then he begins to tell Shermie about tame hamsters. "In 1930, a zoologist in Jerusalem was studying wild hamsters." Michael stops to explain that a *zoologist* (zoe-AHL-uh-jist) is a person who studies animal life. "This zoologist found a hamster tunnel almost eight feet long. He dug and dug until he came to a mother hamster and her babies at the end of the tunnel." These hamsters weren't ordinary brown hamsters, Michael says, but a special golden kind like Winslow. "The professor took the babies back to his university, and those babies had more babies, who had even more babies!"

"And that's how Winslow came to be," interrupts Shermie.

"Right!" says Michael. "All tame hamsters are descended from the professor's wild hamsters."

Winslow seems to be more interested in eating than in hearing about his great-great grandparents. While Shermie and Michael are still talking, the hamster is helping himself to some cookies. He is an acrobat as well as a thief. To steal those cookies, Winslow has quite a climb, but his hard work is worth the effort. Soon Winslow's cheeks are bulging—he looks almost as wide as he is long.

Winslow is now ready to go back to the cage to store all his goodies, but Michael has other plans. "Shermie, would you keep Winslow out and play with him for a while? I'm going to clean his cage." Winslow stores so much food in the bedding of his cage that Michael has to houseclean nearly every day.

While Winslow is performing acrobatics for Shermie, Michael works hard at cleaning out his cage. Because Winslow is a gnawing animal, his cage is made of metal. If the cage were made of wood, Winslow would gnaw his way to freedom in no time. He would chew up the furniture and carpeting in Michael's house as well. Winslow gnaws to keep his *incisors* (in-SI-zuhrs) worn down. Incisors are sharp teeth that would keep growing if Winslow didn't chew on something.

Because Winslow needs to gnaw, Michael gives him dog biscuits to chew on and pieces of old cotton sheet to shred in his cage. Winslow arranges the sheet in a cozy nest and then buries the gnawed dog biscuits in a special hiding place there.

But along comes Michael, who undoes all of Winslow's hard work! Michael removes the old food and replaces some of the sheet to keep Winslow's cage neat and clean. He also puts fresh water in Winslow's water bottle and new hamster food in his dish. When Winslow gets back in his cage, he quickly sets to work putting his nest back in order and burying the food he has in his cheek pouches. After all that hard work, Winslow takes a turn or two on his exercise wheel.

HAMSTER EQUIPMENT

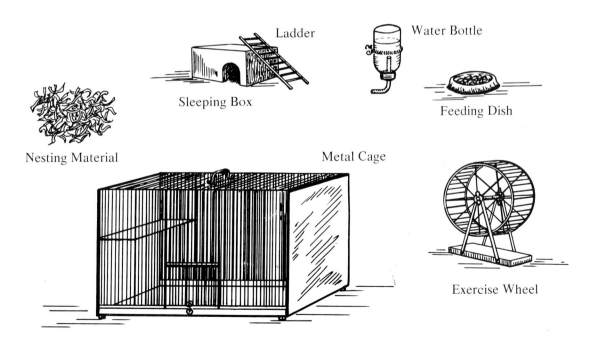

Ladder

Water Bottle

Sleeping Box

Feeding Dish

Nesting Material

Metal Cage

Exercise Wheel

Shermie likes Winslow so much that he decides to get a hamster of his own. So he goes to the Hamster Haven Pet Shop, where he spends all his allowance on one of Winslow's brothers, a golden fellow named Wilbur. Wilbur is a healthy-looking creature with smooth, glossy fur and sparkling clear eyes. The pet shop owner picks Wilbur up by the fur on his neck and cups Wilbur's bottom in his other hand to show Shermie how to handle a hamster. Because Wilbur acts as if he likes being handled, Shermie knows he'll make a good pet.

The pet shop owner says that there are some hamsters who bite and scratch at first. "Until your hamster gets to know you," he says, "be patient with it and win its friendship with sunflower seeds or cookies. You must handle your pet every day and stroke its fur to keep it tame."

Shermie is prepared to win Wilbur's friendship, for he has a whole pocketful of sunflower seeds. After a few minutes of sitting in Shermie's hand and nibbling seeds, Wilbur knows Shermie is his friend. And a few days later Wilbur is quite at home in his new cage. He even feels comfortable nestling near a pair of Shermie's slippers. But Shermie has to watch closely to make sure that Wilbur doesn't start nibbling on them.

Shermie soon decides that his friendly pet is ready to visit Michael's hamster Winslow. But Shermie knows that two hamsters will sometimes fight, even if they are brothers. For that reason, Shermie and Michael are very careful when they bring Wilbur and Winslow together.

Wilbur, who is very curious, inches up to Winslow's cage and puts his nose through the bars. After a few minutes, the two brothers are ready to become friends—they sniff each other and rub noses a little. Soon Wilbur joins Winslow inside his cage for a snack. After that, the two hamsters crawl inside of Winslow's box for a nap.

Shermie tells Michael that hamsters are *nocturnal* animals. "That means they like to roam around at night and sleep during the day." Just as he and Michael turn to leave, one of the hamsters sticks his whiskered nose out as if to say "good night."

But which brother is it—Wilbur or Winslow? Michael shrugs and says, "Come on, Shermie, let's go to the kitchen and fill our own pouches."

# DO YOU KNOW . . .

- what kinds of animals are related to hamsters?

- how hamsters help scientists who study human diseases?

- how many descendants a pair of hamsters could have in one year?

TO FIND THE ANSWERS TO THESE QUESTIONS, TURN THE PAGE

# FACTS ABOUT HAMSTERS

Hamsters belong to the group of animals called *mammals*, whose babies drink their mothers' milk. Hamsters are also members of the *rodent* family, which includes mice, rats, and guinea pigs. Like other rodents, hamsters have a set of gnawing teeth, which keep growing. These gnawing teeth, or incisors, are worn down through constant nibbling. If a pet hamster does not have anything to chew on except soft foods, its teeth will grow so long that it will be unable to eat or to close its mouth.

Mouse

Hamster

Rat

Guinea Pig

**THE HAMSTER AND ITS RELATIVES**

After a few days of cold weather, hamsters go into a kind of sleep called *hibernation*. During this time, a hamster's heart and breathing slow down and its body temperature becomes lower. Medical scientists have studied hamster hibernation to learn more about lowering body temperature and slowing down the heart and breathing in humans during surgery. Hamsters are often used by scientists who want to learn more about health problems in humans.

About 16 days after mating, a mother hamster gives birth to six or seven babies. Do not be alarmed if you see the new mother put one of her babies in her mouth. Hamsters use their mouths for carrying around their young as well as for storing food.

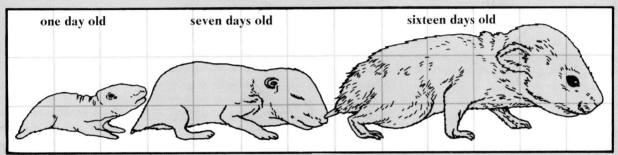

one day old      seven days old      sixteen days old

*Pictures shown actual size (each square = ½ inch).*

Hamster babies are blind and hairless at birth, but they grow very fast. Young hamsters can have babies of their own when they are just seven or eight weeks old. Hamsters have babies so fast that in half a year one pair of hamsters could have 200 descendants. In one year, the number could grow to 100,000 descendants. Because hamsters are such fast breeders, pet owners must take special care to keep their pet hamsters from escaping outdoors. The descendants of an escaped pair could become pests like the wild hamsters that used to bother the farmers in Europe.

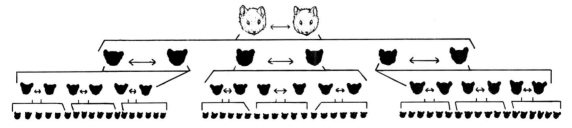

**and so on . . . until there are about 100,000 descendants in one year!**

# *The Animal Friends Books*

Clover the CALF
Jessie the CHICKEN
Ali the DESERT FOX
Splash the DOLPHIN
Dolly the DONKEY
Downy the DUCKLING
ELEPHANTS around the World
Tippy the FOX TERRIER
Marigold the GOLDFISH
Polly the GUINEA PIG
Winslow the HAMSTER
Figaro the HORSE

Rusty the IRISH SETTER
Boots the KITTEN
Penny and Pete the LAMBS
The LIONS of Africa
Mandy the MONKEY
Lorito the PARROT
Curly the PIGLET
Whiskers the RABBIT
Shelley the SEA GULL
Penelope the TORTOISE
Sprig the TREE FROG
Tanya the TURTLE DOVE

## CAROLRHODA BOOKS
241 FIRST AVENUE NORTH — MINNEAPOLIS, MINNESOTA 55401

*Published in memory of Carolrhoda Locketz Rozell,*
*Who loved to bring children and books together*

*Please write for a complete catalogue*